KU-276-187

Ben and Bobo

Written by Martin Waddell
Illustrated by Julian Mosedale

Collins

Ben and Bobo were painting.

Bobo said, "I'm good at painting!"

Ben said, "Mind the lid!"
Bobo said, "What lid?"

Ben said, "Mind the bucket!"
Bobo said, "What bucket?"

Ben said, "Mind the ladder!"
Bobo said, "What ladder?"

Bobo said, "Oh, no!"

10

11

Ben and Bobo looked at the wall.

Ben said, "You *are* good at painting!"

A story map

:paw: Ideas for guided reading :paw:

Learning objectives: read a range of familiar and common words and simple sentences independently; extend their vocabulary, exploring the meanings and sounds of new words; show an understanding of the elements of stories, such as main character, sequence of events, and openings; retell narratives in the correct sequence, drawing on the language patterns of stories

Curriculum links: Personal, Social and

Emotional Development: Work as part of a group or class, taking turns and sharing fairly

High frequency words: and, said, the, at, no, are

Interest words: wallop, splat, crash, bang

Word count: 56

Resources: digital camera, ICT

Getting started

- Look at the front cover together. Discuss what is happening in the picture. Ask children to tell a partner what they can see.

- Read the blurb together, pointing to each word as you read.

- Ask children to share their ideas about what will go wrong in the story.

Reading and responding

- Turn to pp2–3 and read it together.

- Look at the punctuation used on pp2–3, e.g. full stop, comma, speech marks, exclamation mark. Ask children to explain what the marks mean. Reread the sentences, modelling how to read with expression.

- Discuss what is known about Ben and Bobo so far. How are they the same and how are they different, e.g. *Ben is careful and tidy; Bobo is messy.*

- Ask children to read the story aloud to p13, using expression. Support and praise as children read.